W9-BDP-988

WITHDRAWN

No Backbone!
The World of Invertebrates

Squirting Squids

by Natalie Lunis

Consultant: Bill Murphy
Marine Biologist, Northern Waters Gallery
New England Aquarium
Boston, MA

BEARPORT
PUBLISHING

NEW YORK, NEW YORK

Credits

Cover and Title Page, © Doug Perrine/SeaPics.com, © Dennis Sabo/istockphoto, © James D. Watt / SeaPics.com, © Dirscherl Reinhard/Prisma/SuperStock, and © James D Watt/Stephen Frink Collection/Alamy; Title Page © Doug Perrine/SeaPics.com; 4–5, © Prisma/SuperStock; 4 (Background), © Doug Perrine/SeaPics.com; 6, © David Wrobel/SeaPics.com; 7, © David Fleetham/Alamy; 8, © Doc White/SeaPics.com; 9, © 2007 Ned DeLoach/MarineLifeImages.com; 10T, © Brian J. Skerry/National Geographic/Getty Images; 10B, © Fred Bavendam/Minden Pictures; 11, © Bob Cranston/SeaPics.com; 12, © Doc White/naturepl.com; 13, © Ross Land/Getty Images; 14, © John C. Lewis/SeaPics.com; 15, © Doug Perrine/SeaPics.com; 16, © Richard Herrmann/SeaPics.com; 17, © Brian J. Skerry/National Geographic/Getty Images; 18, © AP Images/Tsunemi Kubodera of the National Science Museum of Japan, HO; 19, © 2007 New Zealand Ministry of Fisheries/Getty Images; 21, © National Geographic/SuperStock; 22T, © Stuart Westmorland/Corbis; 22BL, © Chris Newbert/Minden Pictures; 22BR, © Douglas Faulkner/Photo Researchers, Inc.; 22 Spot, © Amir Stern/Shutterstock; 23TL, © Jim Wehtje/Photodisc Green/Getty Images; 23TR, © Mark Conlin/Visual&Written SL/Alamy; 23BL, © Bob Cranston/SeaPics.com; 23BR, © Bruce Coleman Inc./Alamy.

Publisher: Kenn Goin
Editorial Director: Adam Siegel
Creative Director: Spencer Brinker
Design: Dawn Beard Creative
Photo Researcher: Elaine Soares

Library of Congress Cataloging-in-Publication Data

Lunis, Natalie.
  Squirting squids / by Natalie Lunis ; consultant, Bill Murphy.
    p. cm. — (No backbone! : the world of invertebrates)
  Includes bibliographical references and index.
  ISBN-13: 978-1-59716-513-6 (library binding)
  ISBN-10: 1-59716-513-1 (library binding)
  1. Squids—Juvenile literature. I. Title. II. Series.

QL430.2.L86 2008
594'.58—dc22
                          2007012263

For more information, write to Bearport Publishing Company, Inc., 101 Fifth Avenue, Suite 6R, New York, New York 10003. Printed in the United States of America.

10 9 8 7 6 5 4 3

Contents

Boneless Bodies

fins

Squids are animals that live in the sea.

They have two fins, eight arms, and two **tentacles**.

The arms and tentacles look alike.

One thing squids don't have is a **backbone**.

In fact, they don't have any bones at all!

Instead of a backbone, a squid has a hard, hollow tube inside its body. The tube is called a pen. It helps the body keep its shape.

Arrows of the Sea

Some people call squids "sea arrows."

A squid's body is shaped like an arrow.

Also, like an arrow, a squid can move very quickly.

The fastest squids can shoot through the sea at about 25 miles per hour (40 kph).

Some squids can shoot up and out of the water. Sometimes they even land on the decks of boats!

Jetting Away

Sometimes a squid uses its fins or arms to swim slowly.

When it needs to move fast, however, it does something else.

First, it sucks water into two holes near its eyes.

Then it squirts the water out of a tube.

As the water squirts out, the squid jets away.

The tube that a squid uses to squirt out water is called a **siphon**.

siphon

Grabbing and Gripping

suckers

Squids use their arms and tentacles mostly for eating.

They stretch out their long tentacles to catch fish, crabs, shrimp, and other sea creatures.

Then they use their arms to pull the food to their mouths.

Cup-shaped **suckers** on the arms help them keep their grip.

fish

Squids have sharp, parrot-like beaks. They use them to crack hard shells and tear apart food.

beak

Enemies All Around

Squids chase and eat many kinds of animals.

These fast-moving hunters have enemies of their own, however.

Sharks and many other kinds of fish catch and eat squids.

So do sea otters, birds, dolphins, and whales.

sea otter

People have been catching and eating squids for thousands of years.

A Disappearing Act

Squids try to stay safe from enemies.

They are able to change colors to blend in with rocks or plants.

Then their enemies cannot see them.

Some colors that different squids can become are black, gray, orange, and red.

A Squirt of Ink

A squid can also squirt ink out of its siphon to escape from an enemy.

The ink forms a cloud that is shaped like a squid.

The enemy is fooled and attacks the cloud of ink.

Then the real squid makes a quick getaway.

A squid's ink is dark brown.

Monsters of the Deep

There are about 300 kinds of squids.

Some are smaller than a peanut.

The largest ones are rarely seen.

These real-life sea monsters live deep in the ocean.

They can be larger than a city bus.

giant squid

The two largest kinds of squids are the giant squid and the colossal squid.

colossal
squid

Still a Mystery

The sea is full of squids.

After fish and shrimp, they are the most common of all sea creatures.

Yet there is still much to learn about these quick, tricky—and sometimes huge—animals.

Scientists are still discovering new kinds of squids.

Animals that have backbones are known as *vertebrates* (VUR-tuh-brits). Mammals, birds, fish, reptiles, and amphibians are all vertebrates.

Animals that don't have backbones are *invertebrates* (in-VUR-tuh-brits). Worms, jellyfish, snails, and squids are all invertebrates. So are all insects and spiders. More than 95 percent of all kinds of animals are invertebrates.

Here are three invertebrates that are closely related to squids. Like squids, they all live in the ocean.

Octopus

Cuttlefish

Nautilus

Glossary

backbone
(BAK-*bohn*)
a group of
connected bones
that run along
the backs of some
animals, such as
dogs, cats, and fish;
also called a spine

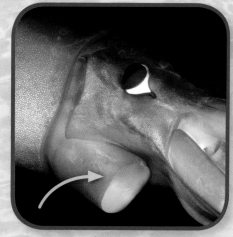

siphon
(SYE-fuhn)
the tube that
a squid uses to
squirt out water
or ink

suckers
(SUHK-urz)
cup-shaped bumps
on a squid's
tentacles and arms
that help the squid
hold on to food

tentacles
(TEN-tuh-kuhlz)
the two long,
arm-like body
parts that a squid
uses to grab food

Index

Read More

Dussling, Jennifer. *Giant Squid: Mystery of the Deep.* New York: Grosset & Dunlap (1999).

Rake, Jody Sullivan. *Squids.* Mankato, MN: Capstone Press (2007).

Redmond, Shirley Raye. *Tentacles!: Tales of the Giant Squid.* New York: Random House Books for Young Readers (2003).

Learn More Online

To learn more about squids, visit **www.bearportpublishing.com/NoBackbone**